PIANO SOLO

2ND EDITION

BROADWAY ★ 20 PIANO SOLOS

W9-AAX-304

ISBN 978-0-634-06423-4

HAL•LEONARD®
CORPORATION
7777 W. BLUEMOUND RD. P.O. BOX 13819 MILWAUKEE, WI 53213

Visit Hal Leonard Online at
www.halleonard.com

ALL I ASK OF YOU
from THE PHANTOM OF THE OPERA

Music by ANDREW LLOYD WEBBER
Lyrics by CHARLES HART
Additional Lyrics by RICHARD STILGOE

Andante

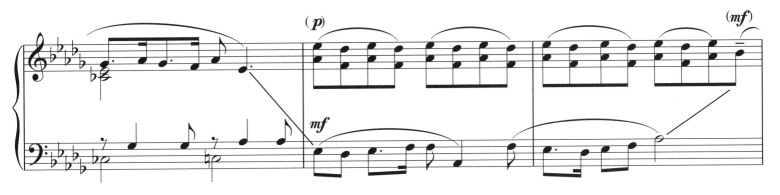

molto rit.   *f* a tempo

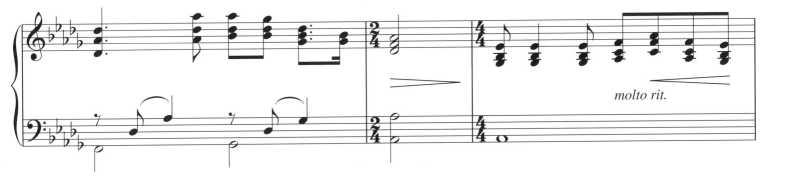

molto rit.

f *a tempo*

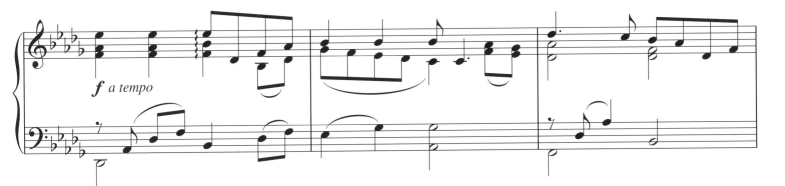

Grandioso

broaden   *ff*

mp   *molto rit.*

8vb ⌟

AND ALL THAT JAZZ

from CHICAGO

Words by FRED EBB
Music by JOHN KANDER

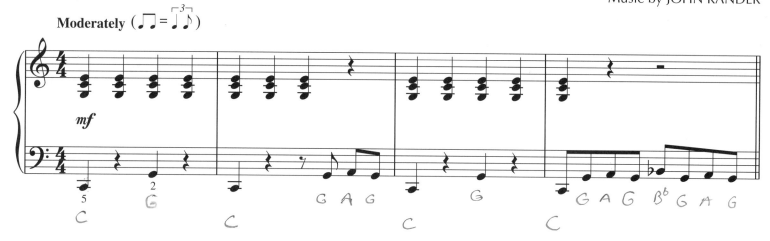

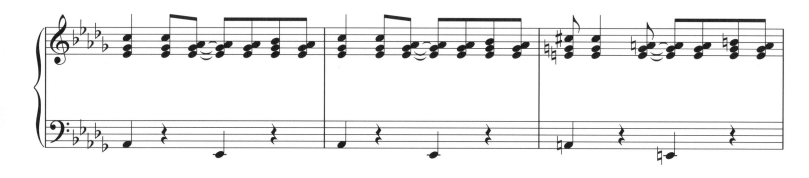

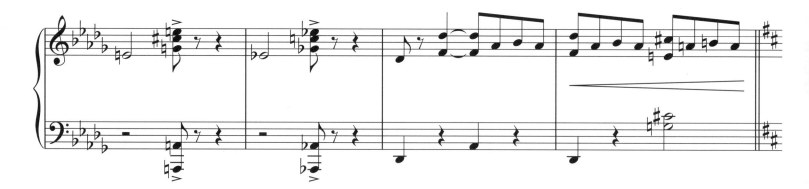

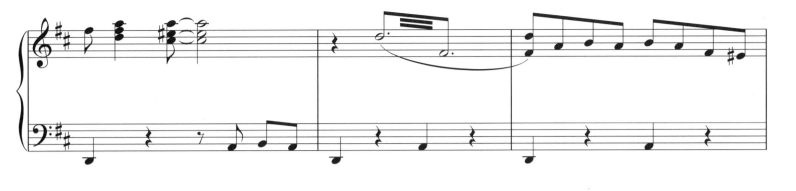

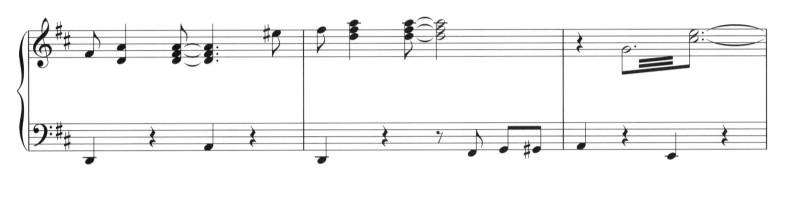

8vb_____

CAN YOU FEEL THE LOVE TONIGHT

Disney Presents THE LION KING: THE BROADWAY MUSICAL

Music by ELTON JOHN
Lyrics by TIM RICE

Freely and expressively

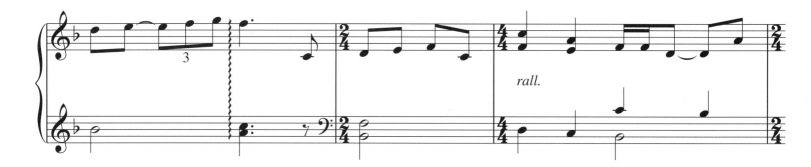

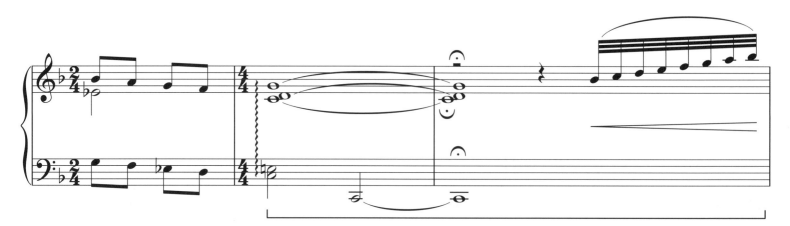

15

Moderately slow

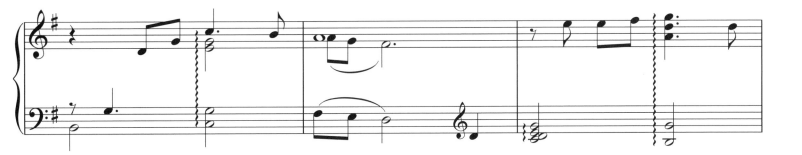

EDELWEISS
from THE SOUND OF MUSIC

Lyrics by OSCAR HAMMERSTEIN II
Music by RICHARD RODGERS

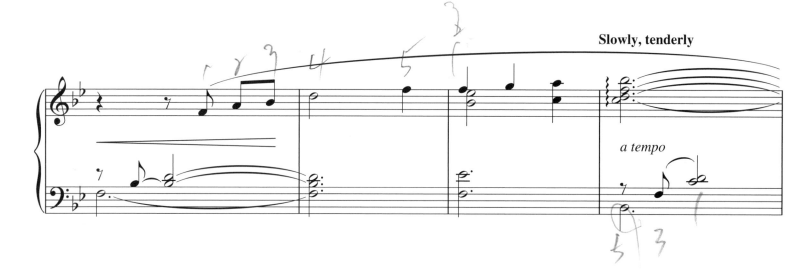

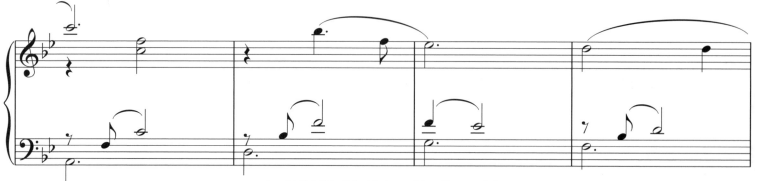

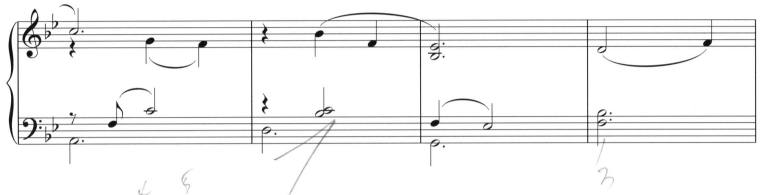

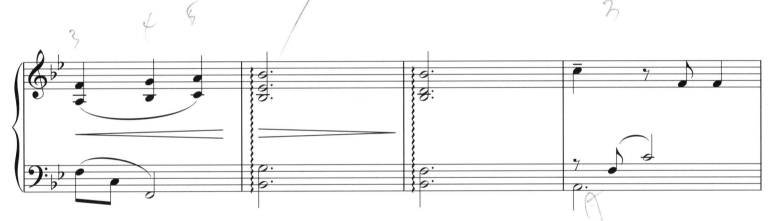

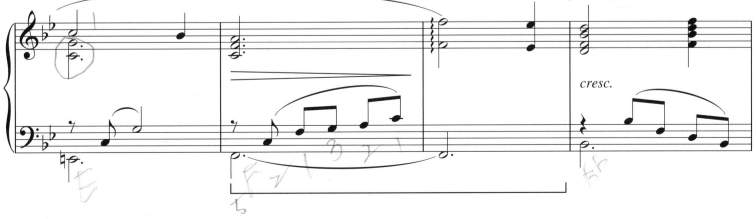

cresc.

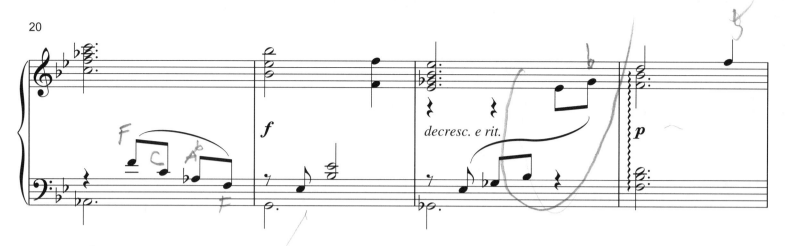

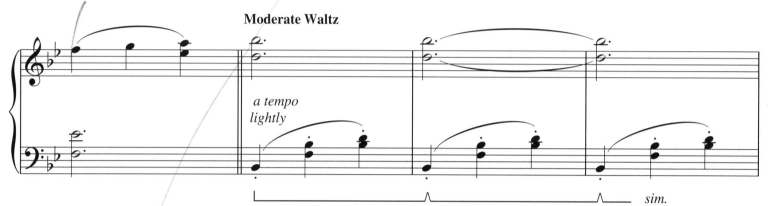

Moderate Waltz

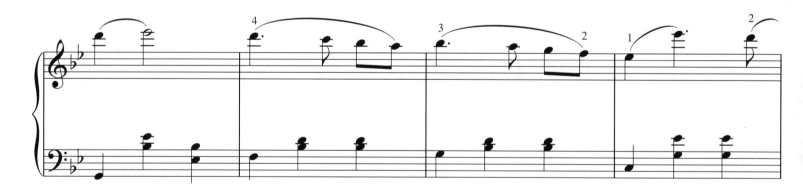

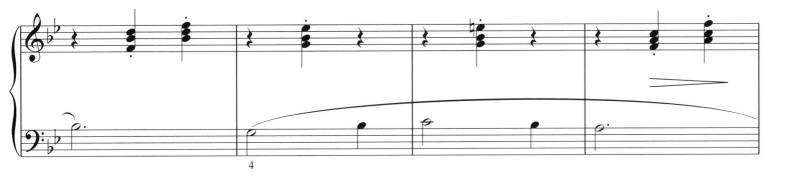

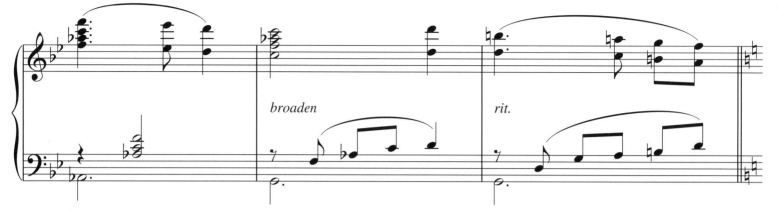

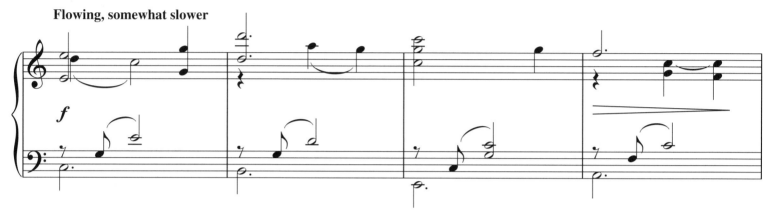

broaden

rit.

Flowing, somewhat slower

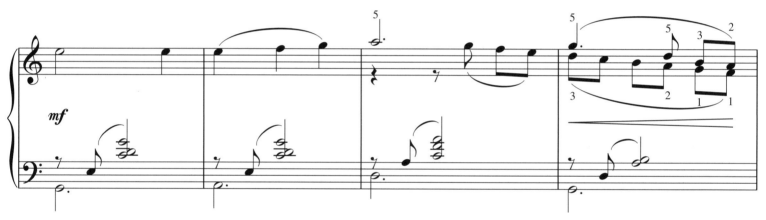

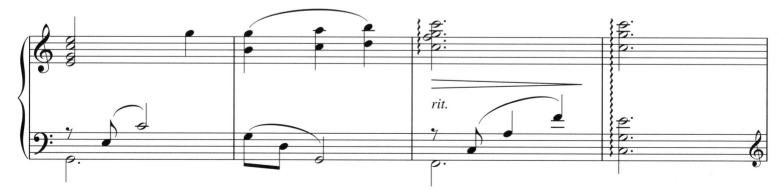

rit.

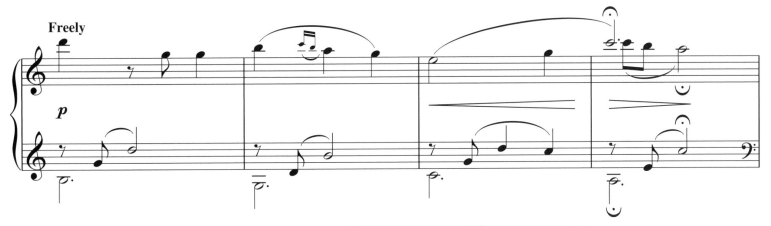

Moderate Waltz

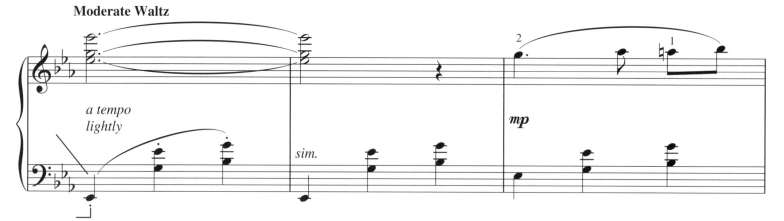

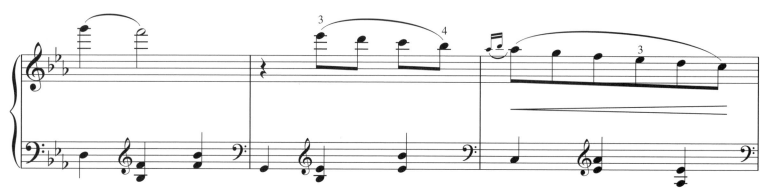

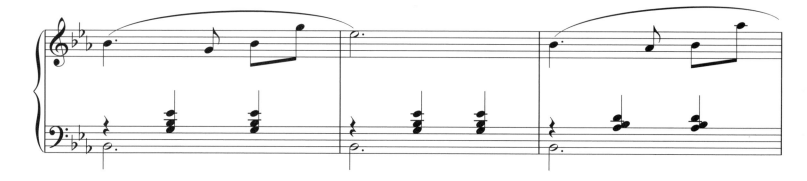

IF I ONLY HAD A BRAIN
from THE WIZARD OF OZ

Lyric by E.Y. "YIP" HARBURG
Music by HAROLD ARLEN

Moderately

I'VE GROWN ACCUSTOMED TO HER FACE

from MY FAIR LADY

Words by ALAN JAY LERNER
Music by FREDERICK LOEWE

Slowly, with feeling

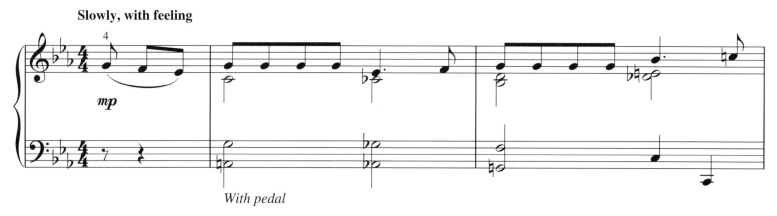

With pedal

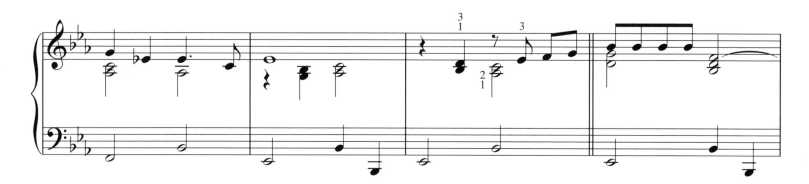

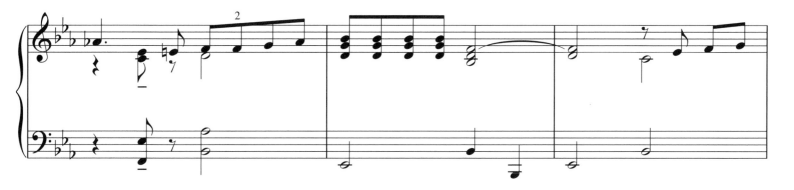

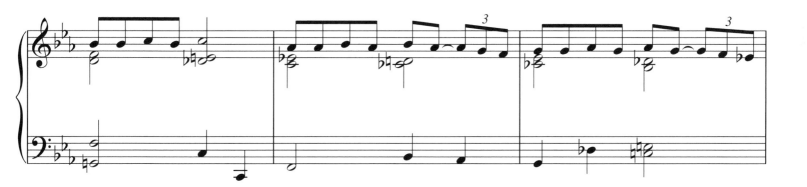

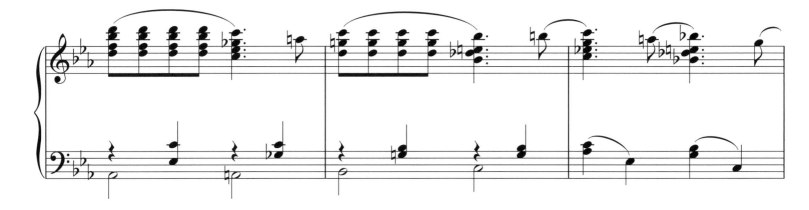

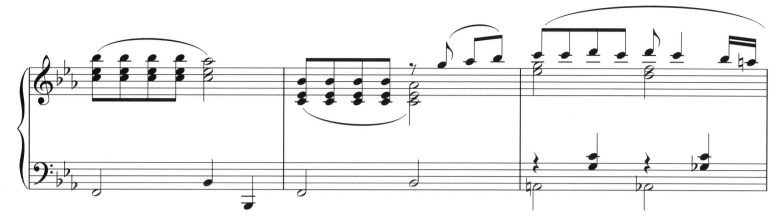

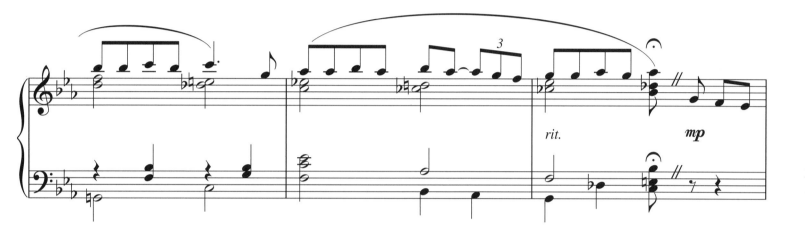

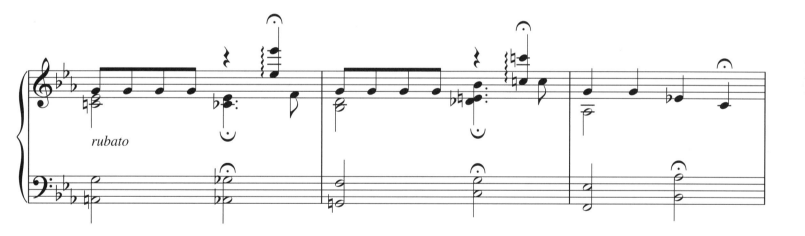

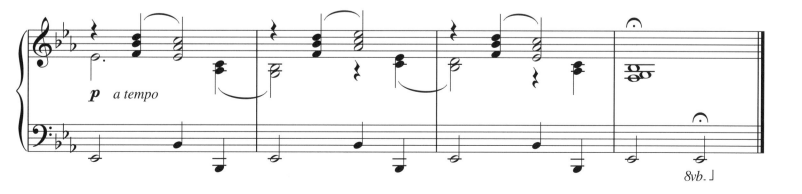

8vb. ⌋

THE IMPOSSIBLE DREAM
(The Quest)
from MAN OF LA MANCHA

Lyric by JOE DARION
Music by MITCH LEIGH

Tempo di Bolero

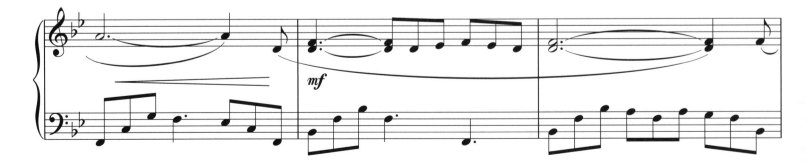

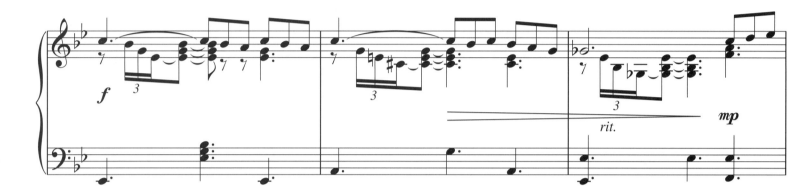

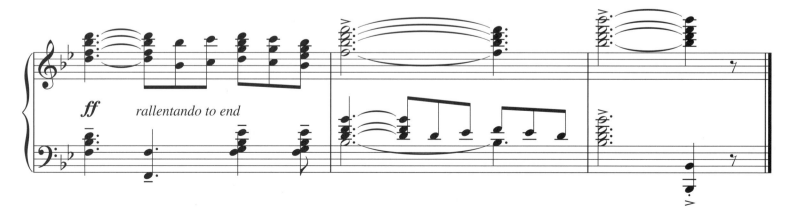

OVER THE RAINBOW
from THE WIZARD OF OZ

Music by HAROLD ARLEN
Lyric by E.Y. "YIP" HARBURG

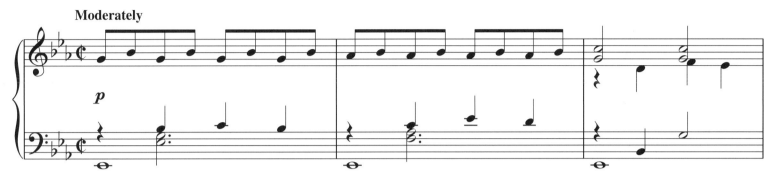

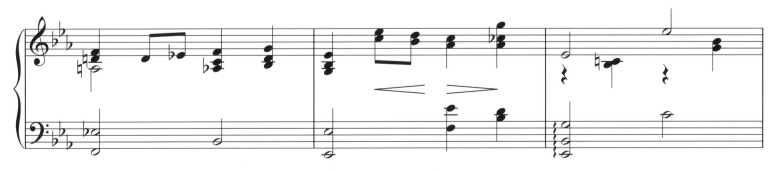

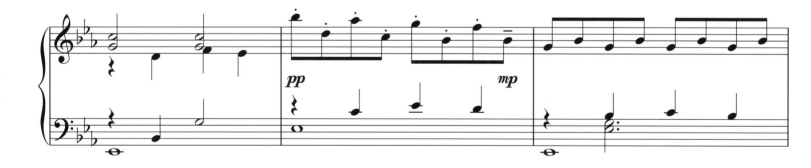

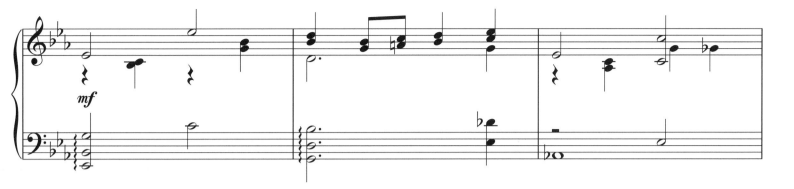

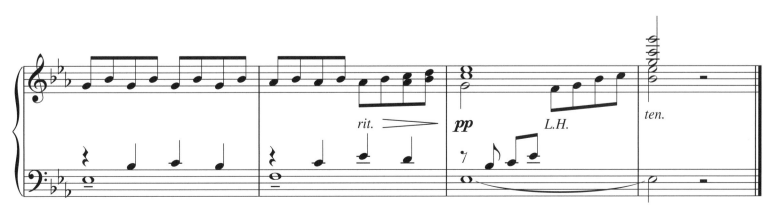

MEMORY
from CATS

Music by ANDREW LLOYD WEBBER
Text by TREVOR NUNN after T.S. ELIOT

Freely and expressively

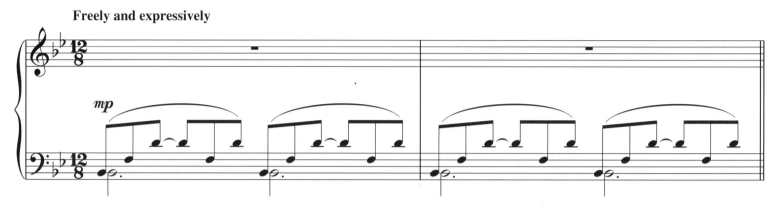

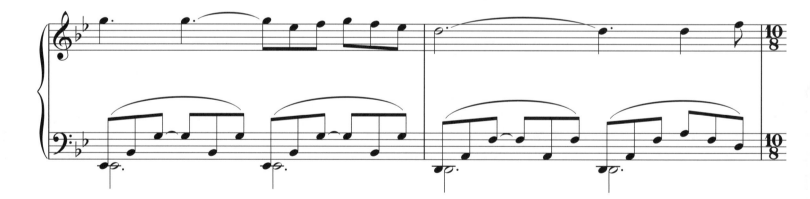

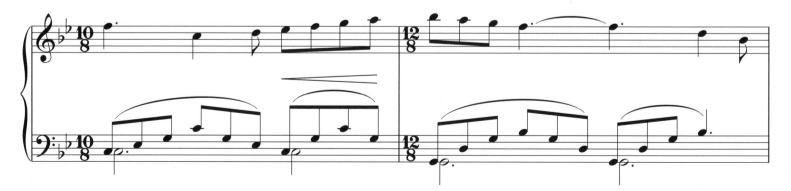

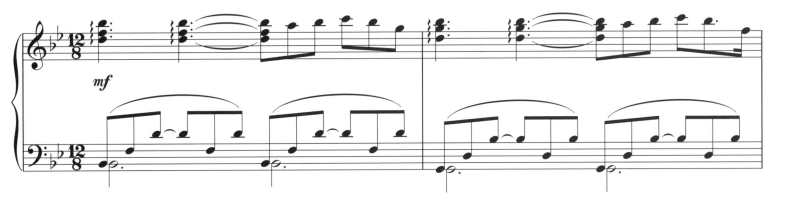

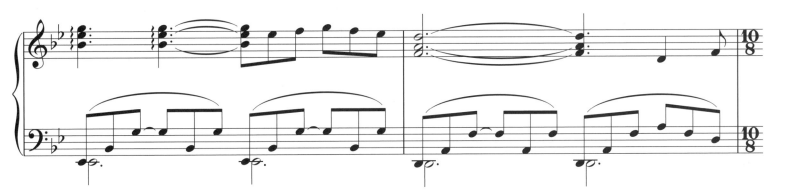

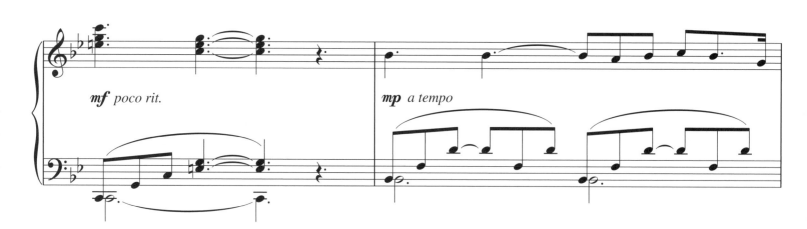

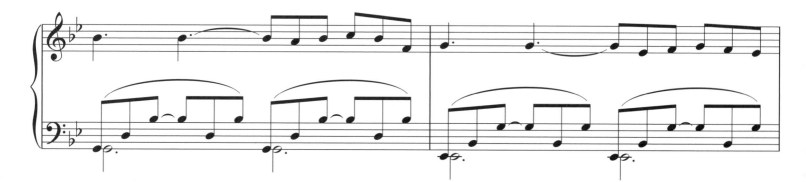

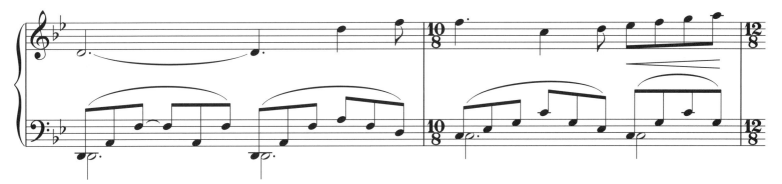

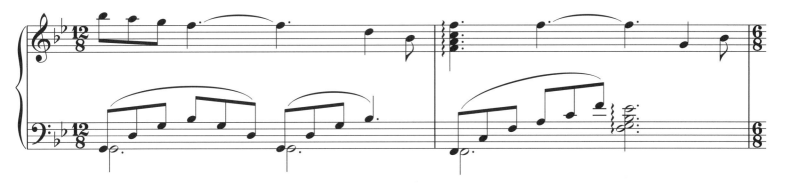

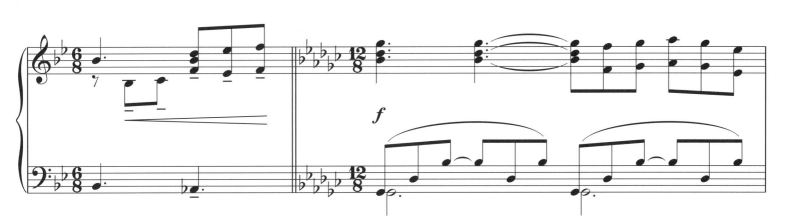

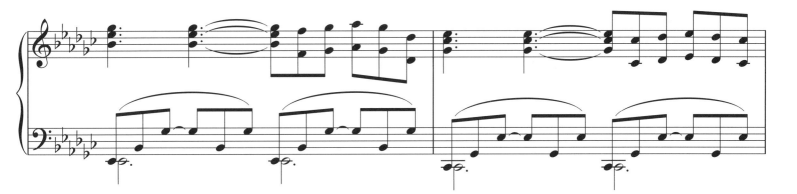

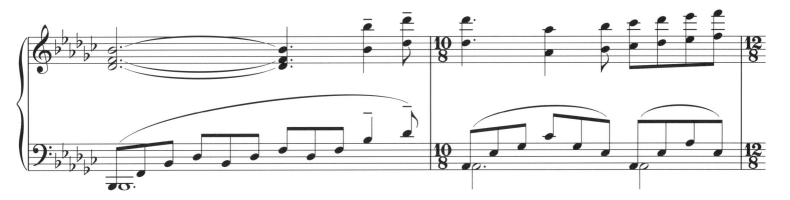

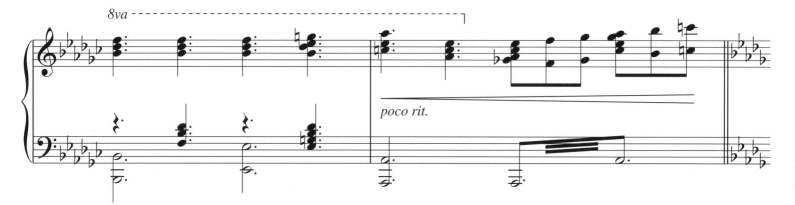

Grandiose

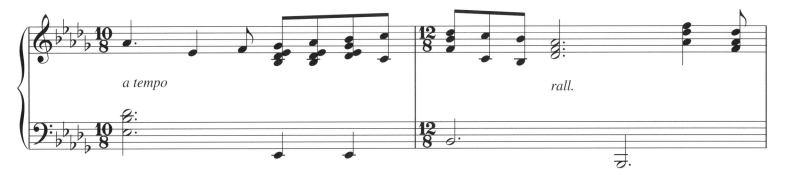

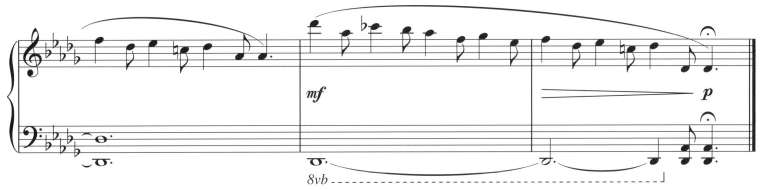

ON MY OWN

from LES MISÉRABLES

Music by CLAUDE-MICHEL SCHÖNBERG
Lyrics by ALAIN BOUBLIL, JEAN-MARC NATEL,
HERBERT KRETZMER, JOHN CAIRD
and TREVOR NUNN

Very slowly, but steadily

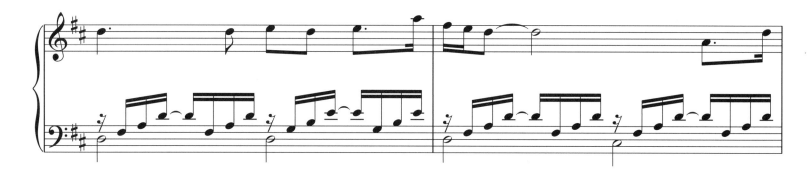

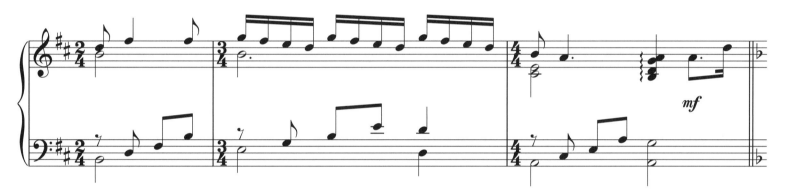

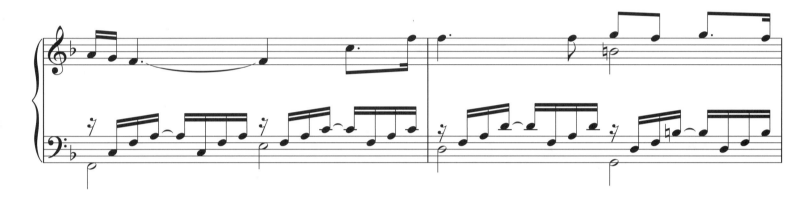

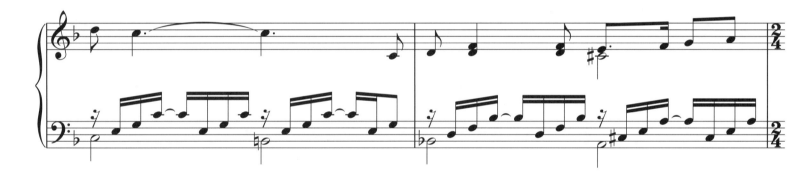

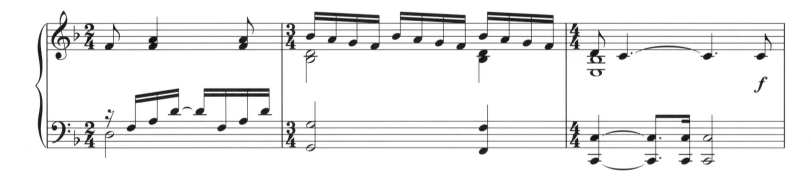

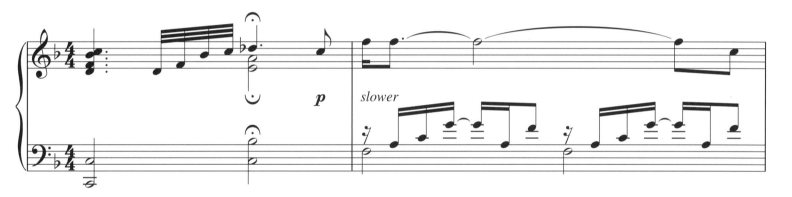

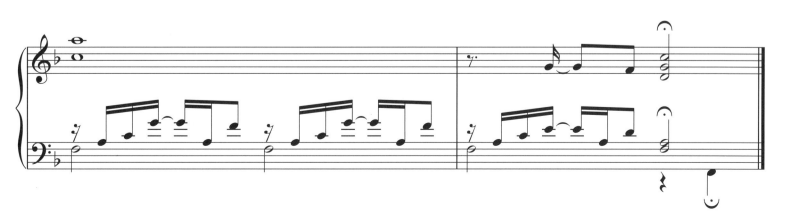

PEOPLE WILL SAY WE'RE IN LOVE
from OKLAHOMA!

Lyrics by OSCAR HAMMERSTEIN II
Music by RICHARD RODGERS

Moderately, in 2

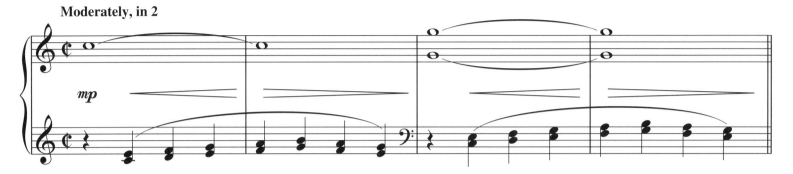

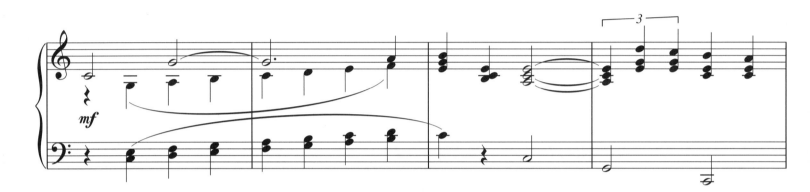

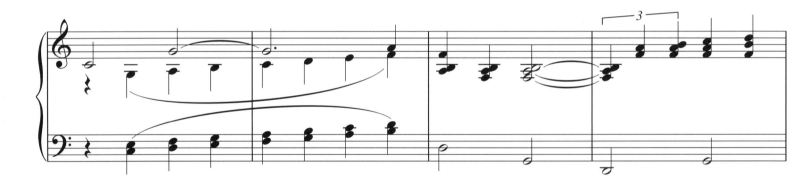

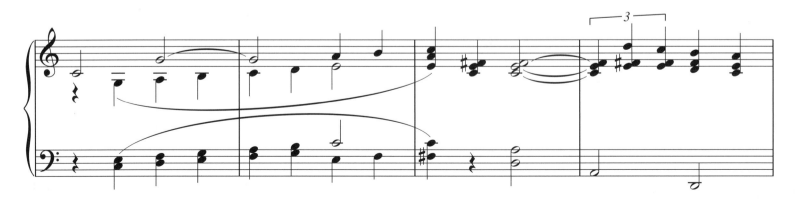

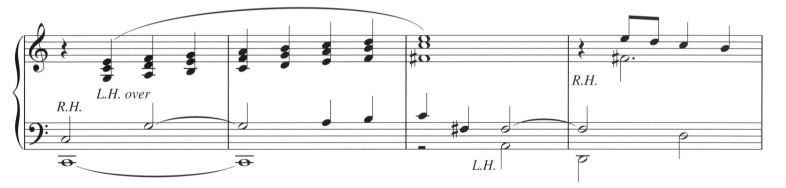

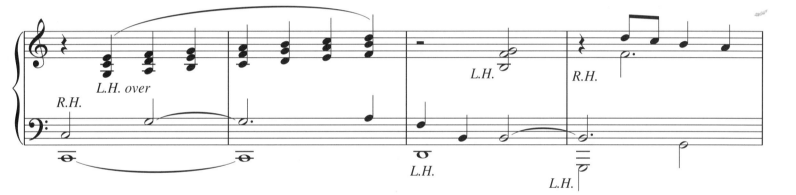

Freely

With motion

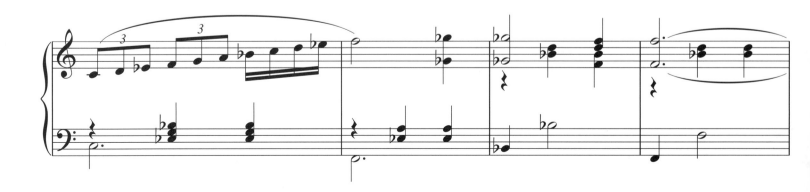

Broadly

Largamente

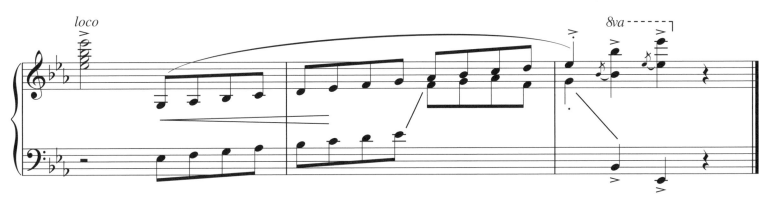

PUT ON A HAPPY FACE
from BYE BYE BIRDIE

Lyric by LEE ADAMS
Music by CHARLES STROUSE

Moderate 2 beat, Swing style

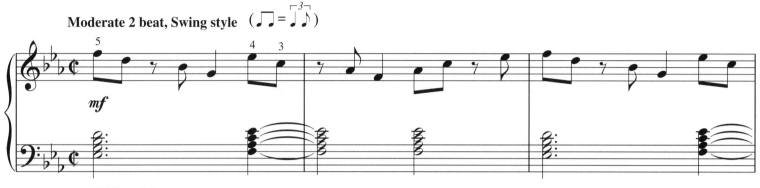

With pedal

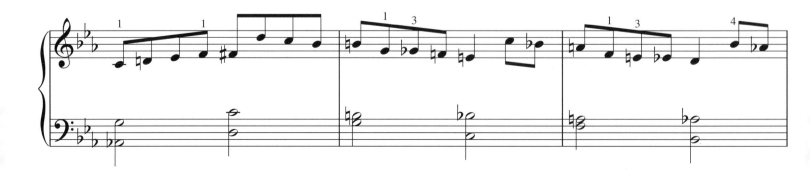

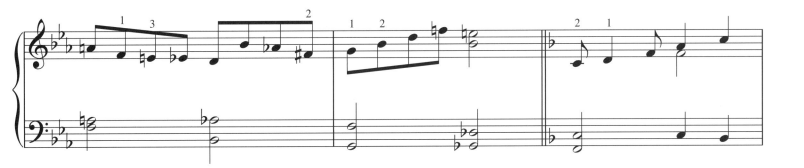

SOME ENCHANTED EVENING

from SOUTH PACIFIC

Lyrics by OSCAR HAMMERSTEIN II
Music by RICHARD RODGERS

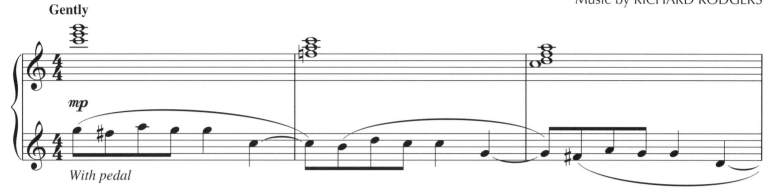

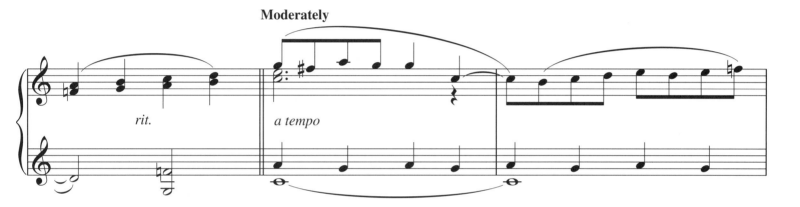

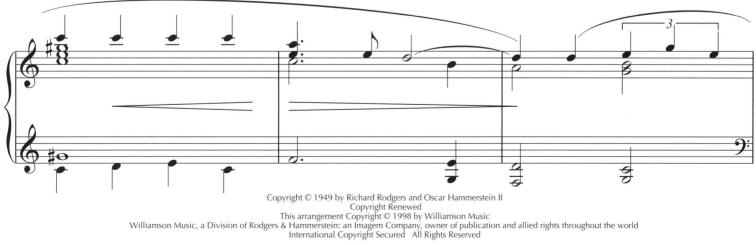

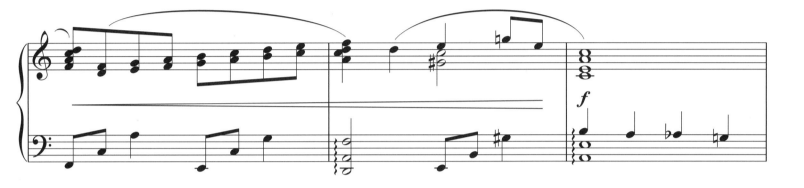

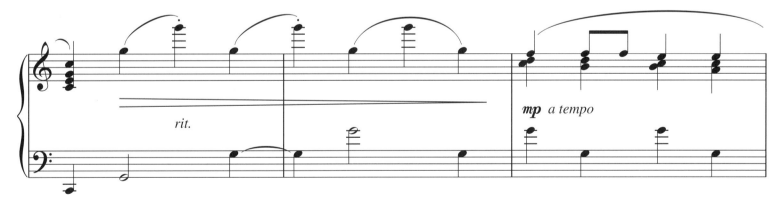

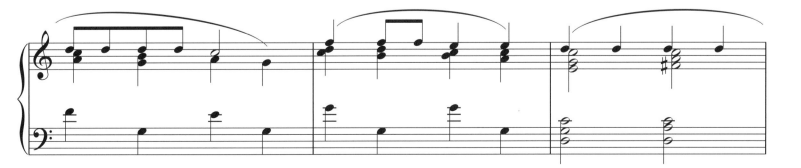

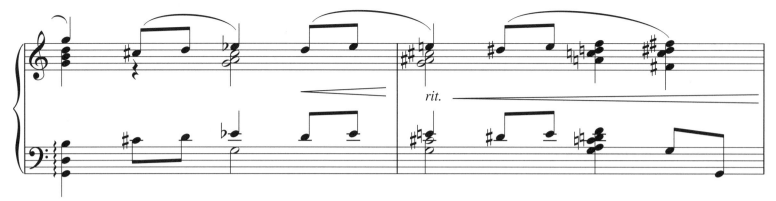

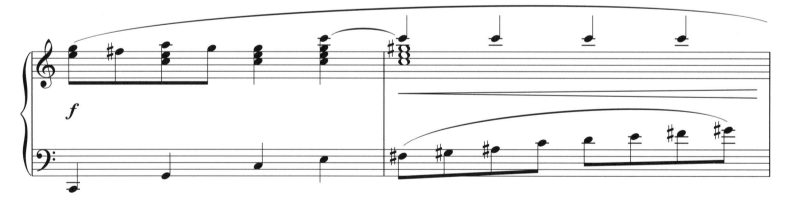

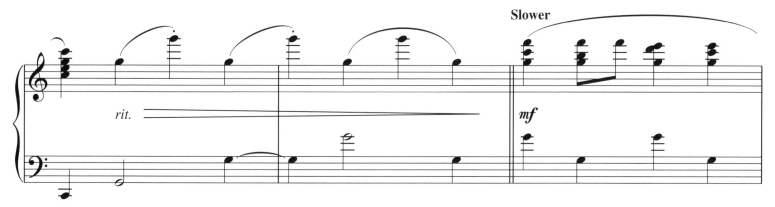

SEASONS OF LOVE

from RENT

Words and Music by
JONATHAN LARSON

Moderate Ballad

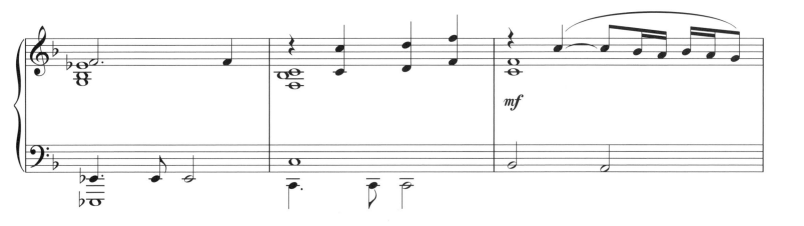

SINGIN' IN THE RAIN
from SINGIN' IN THE RAIN

Lyric by ARTHUR FREED
Music by NACIO HERB BROWN

Moderately

Fine

(melody)

(melody)

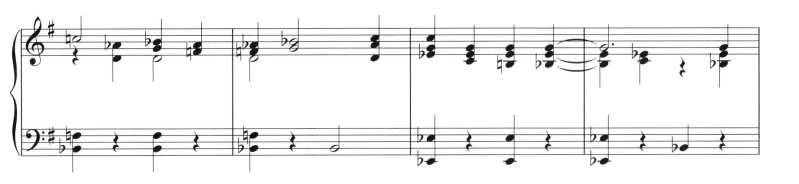

D.S. al Fine

SUMMER NIGHTS
from GREASE

Lyric and Music by WARREN CASEY
and JIM JACOBS

Moderate Rock

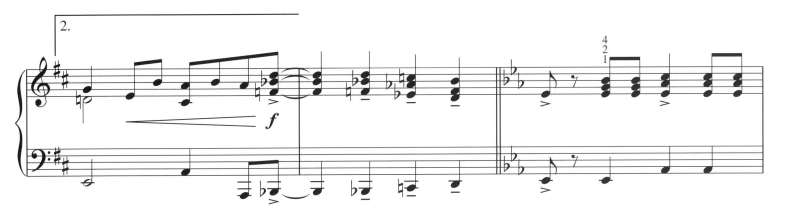

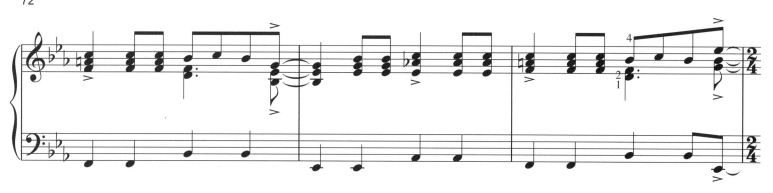

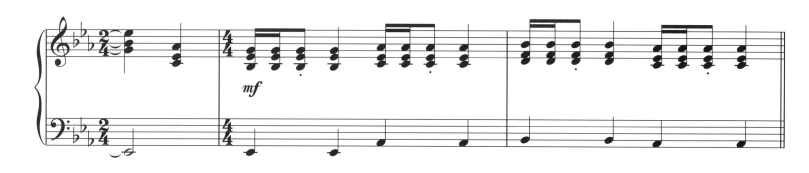

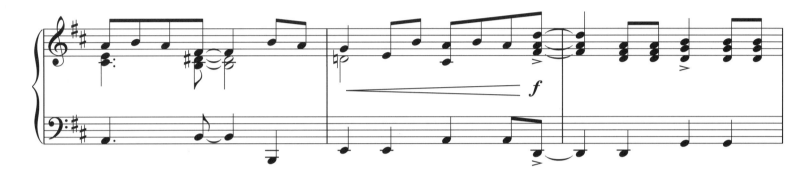

8vb. ♩

UNEXPECTED SONG
from SONG & DANCE

Music by ANDREW LLOYD WEBBER
Lyrics by DON BLACK

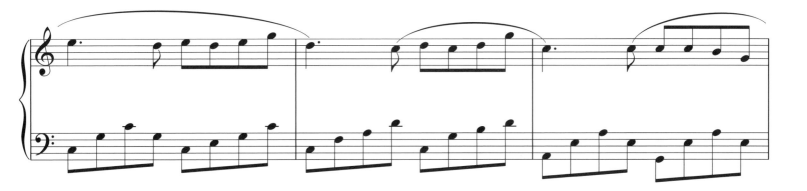

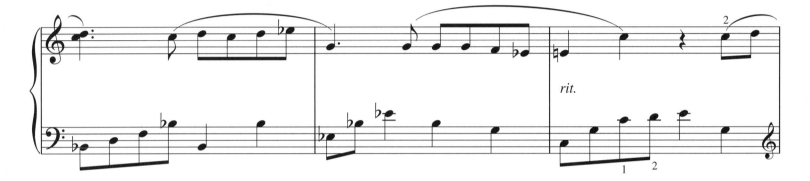

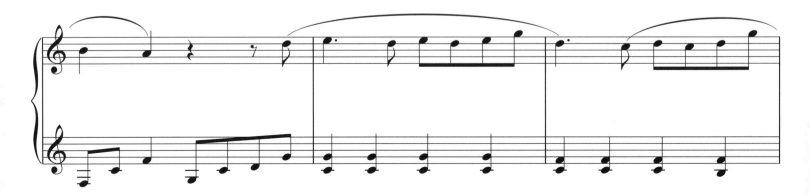

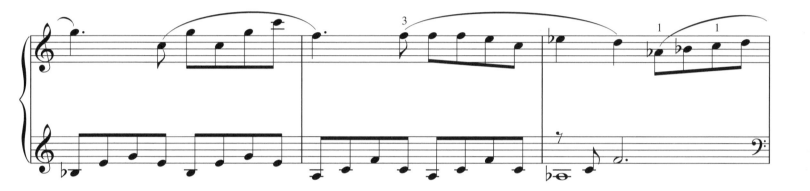

A bit faster

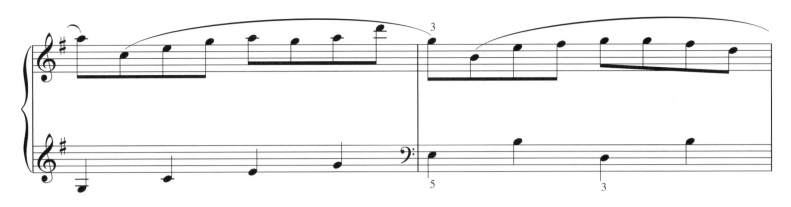

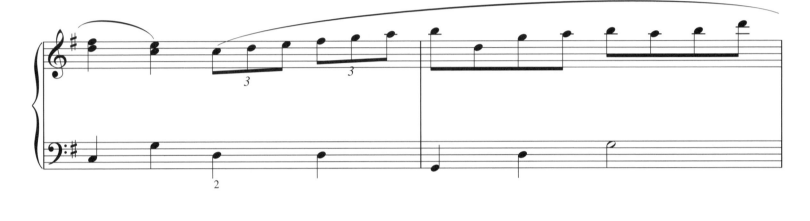

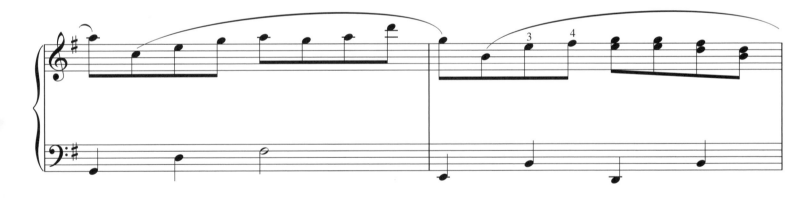

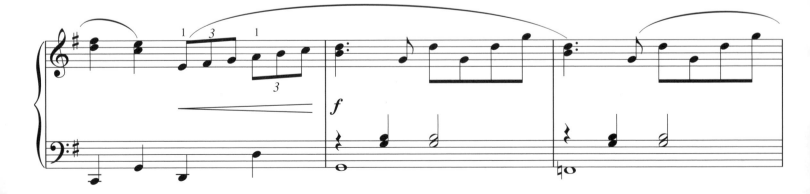

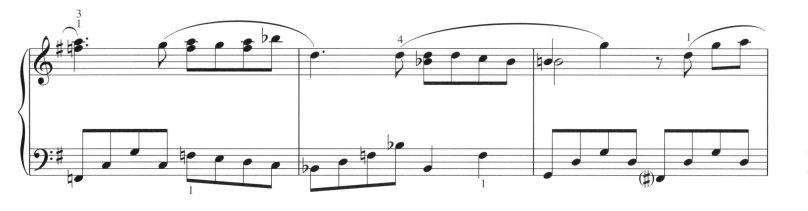

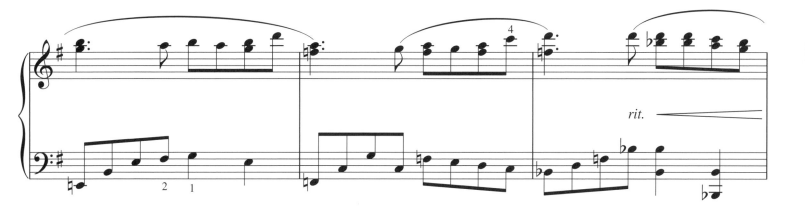

SUN AND MOON

from MISS SAIGON

Music by CLAUDE-MICHEL SCHÖNBERG
Lyrics by RICHARD MALTBY JR. and ALAIN BOUBLIL
Adapted from original French Lyrics by ALAIN BOUBLIL

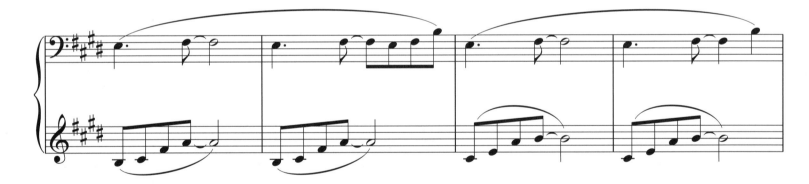

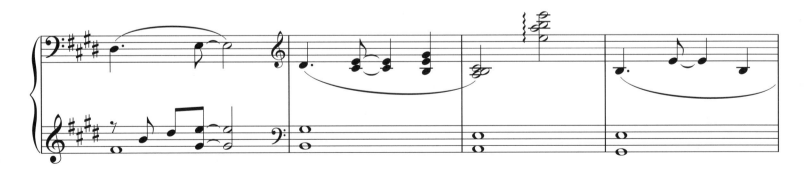

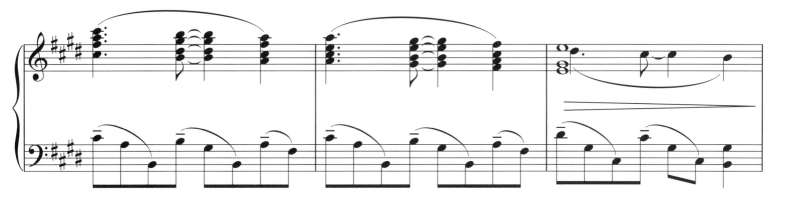

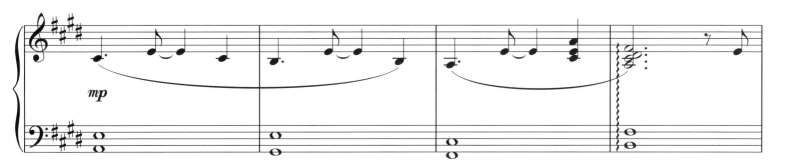

82

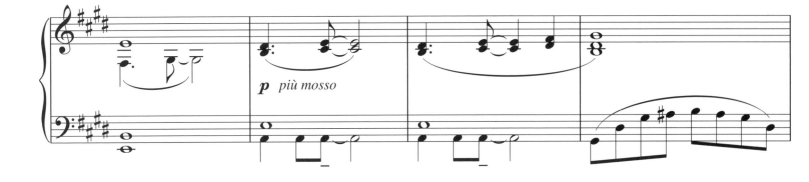

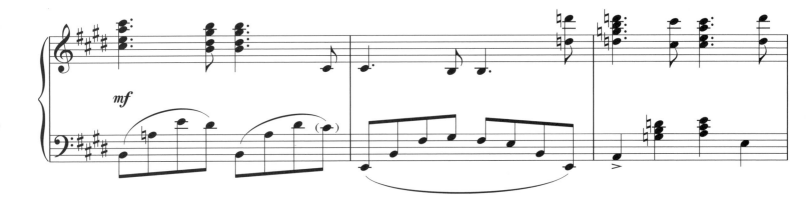

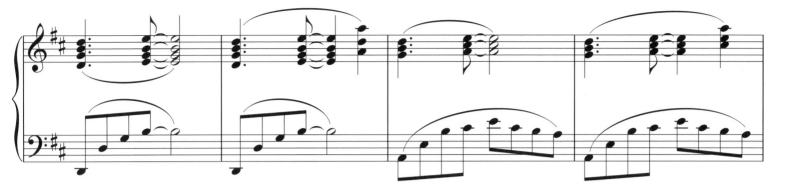

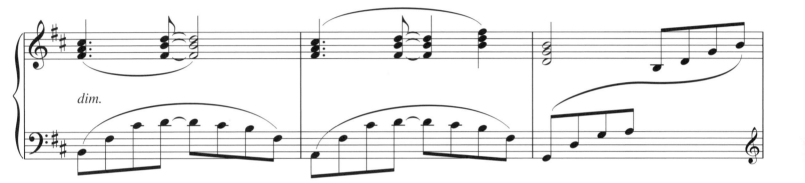

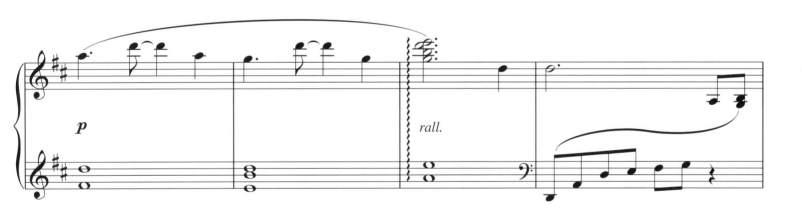

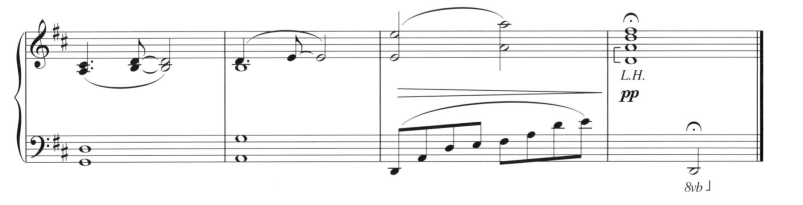

TOMORROW
from the Musical Production ANNIE

Lyric by MARTIN CHARNIN
Music by CHARLES STROUSE

Moderate Ballad

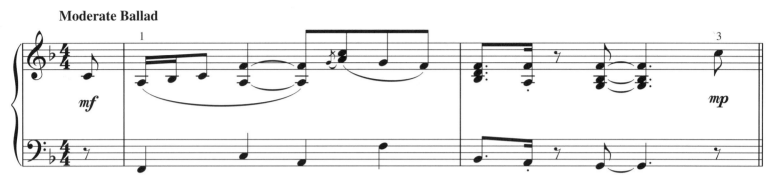

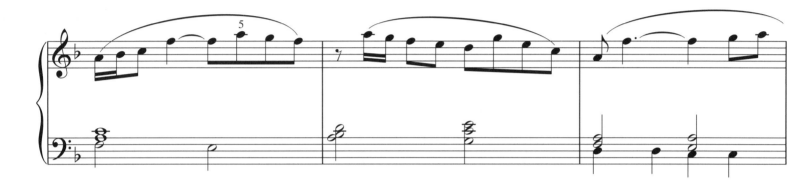

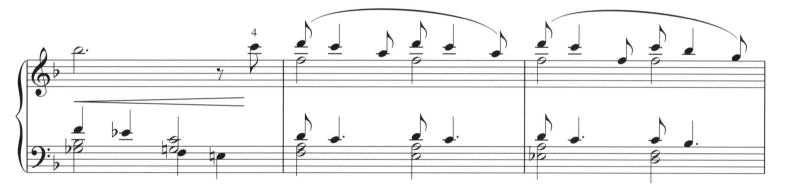

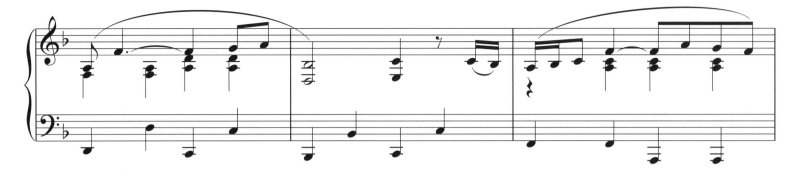

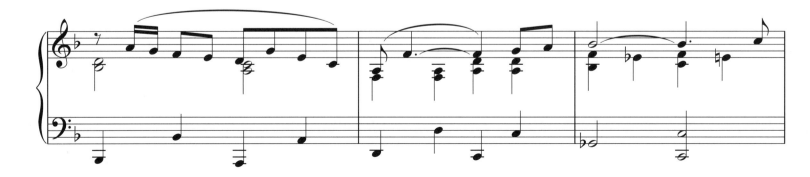

WRITTEN IN THE STARS

from Elton John and Tim Rice's AIDA

Music by ELTON JOHN
Lyrics by TIM RICE

Moderate Ballad

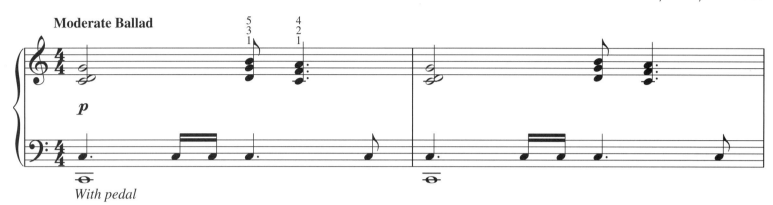

With pedal

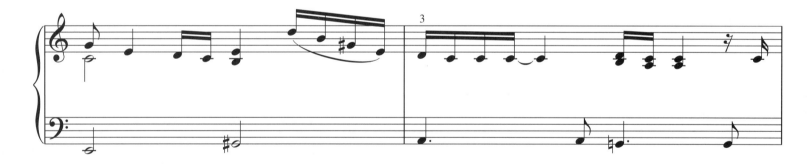

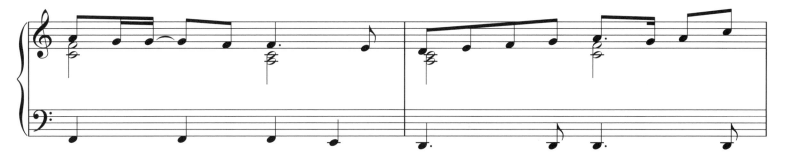

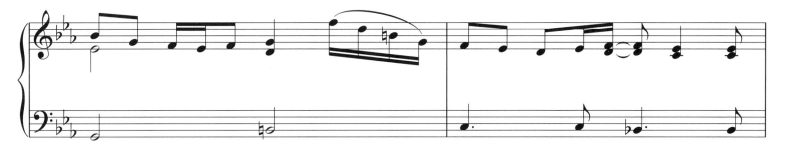

YOUR FAVORITE MUSIC
ARRANGED FOR PIANO SOLO

ADELE FOR PIANO SOLO
This collection features 10 Adele favorites beautifully arranged for piano solo, including: Chasing Pavements • Rolling in the Deep • Set Fire to the Rain • Someone like You • Turning Tables • and more.
00307585 ....$12.99

THE HUNGER GAMES
Music by James Newton Howard
Our matching folio to this book-turned-blockbuster features ten piano solo arrangements from the haunting score by James Newton Howard: Katniss Afoot • Reaping Day • The Train • Preparing the Chariots • Horn of Plenty • The Countdown • Healing Katniss • Searching for Peeta • The Cave • Returning Home.
00316688 ....$14.99

BATTLESTAR GALACTICA
by Bear McCreary
For this special collection, McCreary himself has translated the acclaimed orchestral score into fantastic solo piano arrangements at the intermediate to advanced level. Includes 19 selections in all, and as a bonus, simplified versions of "Roslin and Adama" and "Wander My Friends." Contains a note from McCreary, as well as a biography.
00313530 ....$16.99

PRIDE & PREJUDICE
12 piano pieces from the 2006 Oscar-nominated film, including: Another Dance • Darcy's Letter • Georgiana • Leaving Netherfield • Liz on Top of the World • Meryton Townhall • The Secret Life of Daydreams • Stars and Butterflies • and more.
00313327 ....$14.99

COLDPLAY FOR PIANO SOLO
Stellar solo arrangements of a dozen smash hits from Coldplay: Clocks • Fix You • In My Place • Lost! • Paradise • The Scientist • Speed of Sound • Trouble • Up in Flames • Viva La Vida • What If • Yellow.
00307637 ....$12.99

GEORGE GERSHWIN – RHAPSODY IN BLUE (ORIGINAL)
Alfred Publishing Co.
George Gershwin's own piano solo arrangement of his classic contemporary masterpiece for piano and orchestra. This masterful measure-for-measure two-hand adaptation of the complete modern concerto for piano and orchestra incorporates all orchestral parts and piano passages into two staves while retaining the clarity, sonority, and brilliance of the original.
00321589 ....$14.95

DISNEY SONGS
12 Disney favorites in beautiful piano solo arrangements, including: Bella Notte (This Is the Night) • Can I Have This Dance • Feed the Birds • He's a Tramp • I'm Late • The Medallion Calls • Once Upon a Dream • A Spoonful of Sugar • That's How You Know • We're All in This Together • You Are the Music in Me • You'll Be in My Heart (Pop Version).
00313527 ....$12.99

TAYLOR SWIFT FOR PIANO SOLO
Easy arrangements of 15 of Taylor's biggest hits: Back to December • Fearless • Fifteen • Love Story • Mean • Mine • Our Song • Picture to Burn • Should've Said No • Sparks Fly • Speak Now • The Story of Us • Teardrops on My Guitar • White Horse • You Belong with Me.
00307375 ....$16.99

GLEE
Super solo piano arrangements of 14 tunes featured in *Glee*: As If We Never Said Goodbye • Beautiful • Blackbird • Don't Stop Believin' • Dream On • Fix You • Hello • I Dreamed a Dream • Landslide • Rolling in the Deep • Sway • (I've Had) The Time of My Life • To Sir, With Love • Uptown Girl.
00312654 ....$14.99

TWILIGHT – THE SCORE
by Carter Burwell
Here are piano solo arrangements of music Burwell composed for this film, including the achingly beautiful "Bella's Lullaby" and ten more pieces: Dinner with His Family • Edward at Her Bed • I Dreamt of Edward • I Would Be the Meal • Phascination Phase • Stuck Here like Mom • Tracking • Who Are They? • and more.
00313440 ....$14.99

GREAT PIANO SOLOS
A diverse collection of music designed to give pianists hours of enjoyment. 45 pieces, including: Adagio for Strings • Ain't Misbehavin' • Bluesette • Canon in D • Clair de Lune • Do-Re-Mi • Don't Know Why • The Entertainer • Fur Elise • Have I Told You Lately • Memory • Misty • My Heart Will Go On • My Way • Unchained Melody • Your Song • and more.
00311273 ....$14.95

UP
Music by Michael Giacchino
Piano solo arrangements of 13 pieces from Pixar's mammoth animated hit: Carl Goes Up • It's Just a House • Kevin Beak'n • Married Life • Memories Can Weigh You Down • The Nickel Tour • Paradise Found • The Small Mailman Returns • The Spirit of Adventure • Stuff We Did • We're in the Club Now • and more, plus a special section of full-color artwork from the film!
00313471 ....$14.99

GREAT THEMES FOR PIANO SOLO
Nearly 30 rich arrangements of popular themes from movies and TV shows, including: Bella's Lullaby • Chariots of Fire • Cinema Paradiso • The Godfather (Love Theme) • Hawaii Five-O Theme • Theme from "Jaws" • Theme from "Jurassic Park" • Linus and Lucy • The Pink Panther • Twilight Zone Main Title • and more.
00312102 ....$14.99

Prices, content, and availability subject to change without notice.
Disney characters and artwork © Disney Enterprises, Inc.

HAL•LEONARD® CORPORATION
7777 W. BLUEMOUND RD. P.O. BOX 13819 MILWAUKEE, WI 53213

www.halleonard.com

0812